INVESTIGATIONS

WHERE SCIENCE IS THE LAW AND SCIENTIFIC THINKING RULES!

Electric Current

INVESTIGATIONS

WHERE SCIENCE IS THE LAW AND SCIENTIFIC THINKING RULES!

Electric Current

Adapted by Tom Sibila
from the original television show written and created by
Tom Snyder
Bill Braudis
David Dockterman
Produced by Tom Snyder Productions

Published by Frank Schaffer Publications, Inc.
Illustrated by Bob Thibeault and Kristine Koob
Created by Kent Publishing Services, Inc.
Designed by Signature Design Group, Inc.

FS-33608 Science Court Investigations—Electric Current
ISBN 0-7682-0001-6

I. M. Richman was a very rich, pompous man. He lived in a magnificent mansion set on a beautiful landscape. He was also a very good ping-pong player. For ten years he had been the town's champion. But this year was different. Mary Murray had beaten him, and he was not taking the licking well. In fact, he refused to admit defeat and would not turn the championship trophy over to Mary. His lame excuse of an injury didn't set well with Mary, who came to Richman's house one evening to claim her trophy. As the two competitors walked through the manicured grounds of the mansion arguing, Mary suddenly tripped over a wire that was hidden in the grass.

Totally disgusted, Mary left leaving Richman holding the broken wire. He wondered how he was going to fix the alarm. It was late, and he didn't know where he could get a three-foot piece of wire to make the repair at such a late hour. As he sat on the lawn thinking, his loyal dog Wedgewood began to get impatient and pulled hard on his leash. At first, Richman was irritated with Wedgewood, but then realized that his leash was just the right length to fix the broken wire. He exclaimed, "Wedgewood, that's it. I can use your leash to fix the alarm." He attached the ends of the leash to the broken wire and went back inside the mansion to turn on the power.

Mr. Richman was ready to turn in for the night now that the alarm was fixed. Wedgewood was still upset and barking as Richman put on his nightgown and nightcap. As he was about to reprimand Wedgewood, he finally noticed what Wedgewood was barking about. The light on the alarm was off. He panicked and shouted, "Oh dear. The light is off. That means there's an intruder. Sound the alarm." Wedgewood jumped on a treadmill-like contraption that was attached to loud speakers and began pumping with his legs. The siren started to go off and before long was blaring an awful sound. Suddenly, Doug Savage appeared outside the mansion knocking at the door.

Doug explained that he was walking by and heard the alarm. Richman gladly invited Doug in and began to explain what happened. He told Doug that the "all clear" light went off, and that indicated that someone tried to break in. Doug looked at the light, which was off, and agreed. Richman further explained that he was certain he knew who it was. He accused Mary Murray of breaking into the mansion to try to steal the trophy. Doug was very surprised and asked Richman if he was sure. Richman said he was positive and persuaded Doug to take his case to prosecute Mary in Science Court.

Doug quickly made a phone call to Julie Bean, science expert, and she came right over. Doug asked her to examine the alarm system and determine if it was effective. She said that it was. She explained how it worked by drawing a diagram of the estate showing a wire running around it. She explained that electricity has to travel in a full circle from a power source, such as a battery, through a wire to an appliance, such as a light bulb, and then back through the wire to the power source. That's called a "complete circuit." She then explained that if the circuit was broken, it would no longer be complete, and the alarm would be off. That was all Doug needed to hear.

Make your own complete electric circuit. Try activity #1 on page 19.

A CIRCUIT CAN BE BROKEN AT THE MAIN SWITCH. WHEN THE SWITCH IS OPEN, THE CIRCUIT IS NOT COMPLETE AND THE LIGHT IS TURNED OFF. ANOTHER WAY THE CIRCUIT CAN BE BROKEN IS FOR AN INTRUDER TO TRIP ON THE WIRE AND BREAK IT. THEN THERE IS NO LONGER A COMPLETE CIRCUIT.

WELL, THAT'S WHAT HAPPENED. THE WIRE WAS BROKEN AND MY LIGHT BULB TURNED OFF.

MR. RICHMAN, I THINK WE ARE READY FOR SCIENCE COURT!

←ALARM LIGHT

←MAIN SWITCH

Sure enough, Doug set the wheels in motion in Science Court, and Mary Murray was charged with attempting to break into Richman's mansion. When Mary learned of the charge, she immediately went to Alison Krempel, famous Science Court attorney, for help. Alison tried to size up Mary by explaining to her how serious the charges were. Mary understood and pleaded her innocence. As further proof, she explained that Mr. Richman's alarm system wasn't even working. She recounted the day she spent at the Richman estate and told Alison about the wire that she accidentally broke. Alison believed Mary and decided to take her case.

It was a typical day in Science Court. Jen Betters, the local news reporter, was ready to watch the trial and report on the proceedings. Alison, Tim, and Mary were seated at the table. Doug and Mr. Richman were also there. Wedgewood and Micaela, a regular at Science Court, had already hit it off and Wedgewood was licking Micaela's face. The jury was ready and Stenographer Fred instructed everyone to rise for the Honorable Judge Stone. The trial began with Judge Stone asking the attorneys for opening statements.

GOOD PEOPLE OF THE JURY, MY CLIENT DID NOT TRY TO ROB MR. RICHMAN OF HIS TROPHY OR ANYTHING ELSE. WE WILL SHOW THAT THE EVIDENCE IS MERELY CIRCUMSTANTIAL AND DOESN'T PROVE ANYTHING.

LADIES AND GENTLEMEN OF THE JURY, THIS CASE IS ABOUT SCIENCE. OH, SURE, I MAY NOT HAVE AN EYEWITNESS, OR ANY EVIDENCE TO ACTUALLY PROVE THAT IT WAS MARY MURRAY WHO TRESPASSED ONTO MR. RICHMAN'S ESTATE AND TRIED TO STEAL HIS PING-PONG TROPHY. BUT, WHAT I DO HAVE IS A BURGLAR ALARM AND A MOTIVE. THE BURGLAR ALARM IS PRACTICALLY FOOLPROOF, AND THE MOTIVE IS JEALOUSY. THANK YOU.

Doug called his first witness to the stand. It was Mary Murray. He asked Mary if she wanted Richman's trophy and she said she certainly felt he should have turned it over to her, since she beat him. He asked her if she could prove where she was on the night of the alleged crime. Mary could not prove that she was at home. He also asked her about a comment she made to Richman. Then, Doug called I. M. Richman to the stand. Mr. Richman explained that the burglar alarm detected an intruder on Saturday at 9:23 PM.

MARY, ISN'T IT TRUE THAT YOU TOLD MY CLIENT YOU WERE GOING TO STEAL HIS TROPHY?

WELL, YES, BUT I WAS ONLY KIDDING. IT WAS A JOKE.

THE TRIP WIRE WHICH RUNS AROUND THE ESTATE WAS BROKEN AND THE "ALL CLEAR" LIGHT IN MY BEDROOM WENT OFF. WHEN I SAW THAT IT WAS OFF, I LOOKED AT THE CLOCK AND IT READ 9:23 PM.

The evidence was mounting against Mary. Doug was doing a surprisingly un-Doug-like good job of presenting his case to the jury. Alison seemed worried and not quite sure what to do next. Tim, her young assistant, had an idea and pleaded with Alison to allow him to cross-examine Mr. Richman. Alison was hesitant but agreed to let Tim try. The results were disastrous and Alison was really in trouble. She asked Judge Stone for a recess so she could regroup.

Alison about blew her fuse. Find out how a fuse works with activity #3 on page 21.

11

Alison was really down. She was afraid she was going to lose her first case. Tim left the courtroom dejected. Doug was beaming at his good fortune and decided to call to the stand Dr. Julie Bean. Doug asked Julie to describe the alarm system at Richman's estate for the jury. She explained that the system involved a wire that lets an electric current flow around the entire estate. If the wire is ever broken, a light in Richman's bedroom turns off so he can be alerted that an intruder is there. Doug had no more questions, so Alison asked Julie to explain how it was possible for electricity to be flowing around the estate. Julie explained that everything in the universe was made up of atoms and molecules which contain electrons.

Alison was even more depressed after Dr. Bean's testimony. Just then, Tim burst into the courtroom and was very excited. He had just come back from an inspection at the Richman estate and found something very interesting. He quietly whispered into Alison's ear what he had found. With new-found energy, Alison asked Judge Stone if the trial could be moved to the site of the alleged crime—the Richman estate. Judge Stone agreed, and they all moved outside to the estate. Once there, Alison called Professor Parsons to testify. Alison let Tim question the professor who was seated in one of the trees on the estate.

PROFESSOR PARSONS, HERE IS A PIECE OF WIRE USED IN MR. RICHMAN'S BURGLAR ALARM SYSTEM. CAN ELECTRONS GO THROUGH THIS WIRE?

OH, YES. THIS IS VERY GOOD COPPER WIRE. ELECTRONS WILL FLOW RIGHT THROUGH THIS BABY.

You can make your own burglar alarm. See activity #2 on page 20.

Confidently, Tim asked the professor another question. He threw up the leash that Richman used to repair the system and asked Professor Parsons if electrons would flow through it. Professor Parsons decided to test it first before answering the question. He pulled out a galvanometer which is a machine that measures how many electrons flow through something. He first tested the copper wire to demonstrate to the jury how it worked. The galvanometer indicated that a lot of electrons were flowing through the copper wire. He then tested the leash. Doug was not pleased with what he heard.

14

RUBBER IS A BAD CONDUCTOR OF ELECTRICITY. IN FACT, IT'S USED TO PROTECT WIRES FROM LEAKING ELECTRICITY. IT'S CALLED "ELECTRICAL INSULATION."

SO, BY ATTACHING THE LEASH TO THE WIRE, MR. RICHMAN DID NOT CREATE A "COMPLETE CIRCUIT" WHICH WAS WHY HIS "ALL CLEAR" LIGHT WAS OFF.

ELECTRICAL INSULATION (RUBBER)

WIRE

THAT'S CORRECT. THE LIGHT TURNED OFF EARLIER IN THE DAY WHEN MARY TRIPPED AND BROKE THE WIRE. MR. RICHMAN SIMPLY DID NOT NOTICE IT UNTIL LATER THAT NIGHT.

Doug challenged Professor Parson's testimony by saying that the leash was made of wire and contained millions of electrons. The professor agreed that there were millions of electrons in the leash, but said that there was a little problem and a big problem. The little problem was that the leash was made of a material whose atoms do not hop around too easily. It was not a good "conductor" of electricity like copper. The big problem was that the leash was covered in rubber.

Needless to say, Alison was very proud of Tim. Judge Stone ordered everyone back to the courtroom for closing arguments. When they reassembled, there was quite a commotion. The jury was mumbling and

Judge Stone ordered quiet in the courtroom. Doug was rattled, and I. M. Richman was very upset at Doug. Alison, Tim, and Mary sat confidently at their table as Doug stood up to deliver his final argument.

LADIES AND GENTLEMEN OF THE JURY, YOU HAVE BEEN A GREAT JURY. REMEMBER THE TIME YOU ALL MUMBLED WHEN SOMEBODY SAID SOMETHING? THAT WAS GREAT. MARY'S GUILTY. AND REMEMBER THE THING WITH THE THING AND EVERYBODY WAS THERE? THANK YOU.

VERY SUBTLE, DOUG. MS. KREMPEL, YOUR CLOSING ARGUMENTS, PLEASE!

Quiz you friends with an electric game you can make yourself. See activity #5 on page 23.

Despite all the twists and turns in the trial, the jury came back with a verdict rather quickly. Stenographer Fred alerted all parties involved to convene back in the courtroom. Once seated at the bench, Judge Stone asked the jury members if they had reached a verdict. The jury foreperson responded that they had.

FORENSIC LABORATORY

What You Need:

- 2 light bulbs, 6-volts each
- 2 light sockets (mini cleat receptacle)
- 3 feet of insulated wire
- 6-volt battery

What You Do:

First

1. Cut the wire into three equal lengths.
2. Strip off about a half inch of the insulation from both ends of the wires.
3. Attach a wire to each of the two screws that are on the light socket.
4. Attach the other end of one wire to the battery terminal. A paper clip works well to clamp the wire to the battery.
5. Attach the end of the remaining wire to the other battery terminal and observe the light bulb.

Next

1. Disconnect one wire from the battery terminal and connect it to the screw on the second light socket.
2. Take another piece of wire and connect it to the other screw on the second light socket.
3. Attach another wire to the battery terminal and observe what happens.

1. Making Circuits — How Do Electric Circuits Work?

What Happens:

When you connect the wires to the battery the light bulb lights up.

What It Proves:

Electricity flows in one direction from the battery through the wires and light bulbs. This is called an electric circuit. As long as the circuit is complete, electricity will flow. If the circuit is broken, electricity will not be able to flow, and the light bulbs will not light.

2 Theft Proof

Can You Make Your Own Burglar Alarm?

What You Need:

- thin cardboard
- aluminum foil
- tape
- 4 feet of insulated wire
- light socket (mini cleat receptacle)
- 6-volt light bulb
- 6-volt battery

What You Do:

First

1. Cut a piece of cardboard about 3 inches by 6 inches and fold it in half.
2. Wind 1-inch strips of aluminum foil around the middle of each cardboard half, and secure with tape.
3. Cut three equal lengths of wire.
4. Strip off about a half-inch of insulation from the ends of each wire.
5. Attach a wire to each piece of aluminum foil with tape.
6. Attach one of the free ends to a screw on the light socket. Attach the other to a battery terminal.
7. Attach a third wire from the remaining screw on the light socket to the remaining battery terminal.

Next

1. Fold the cardboard so that the two pieces of aluminum foil are not touching.
2. Place the folded cardboard under a rug in front of a door. Be sure the two pieces of foil do not touch each other when placed under the rug, but will when someone steps on them.

3. Wait for someone to come through the door and observe the light bulb.

What Happens:

When a person steps on the rug, the cardboard collapses and the two pieces of aluminum foil touch each other. This causes the light bulb to go on.

What It Proves:

Electricity flows through a circuit. When the circuit is broken, electricity cannot flow. The light bulb does not go on until someone steps on the cardboard, and the aluminum foil pieces touch each other. This completes the circuit, allowing the electricity to light the bulb.

3 Circuit Breaker

What Is a Fuse?

What You Need:
- steel wool
- small piece of wood
- 2 pins
- 2 insulated wires
- 6-volt battery

What You Do:
1. Pull out one long strand of steel wool and secure it to the wood by wrapping the ends around pins stuck in the wood. Leave a piece extending from each end.
2. Attach wires to the terminals of the battery.
3. With the free ends of both wires, touch the ends of the strand of steel wool.
4. Observe the strand of steel wool.

What Happens:
The strand of steel wool heats up and glows red hot. It may also melt and break.

What It Proves:
Electricity flows easily through copper wire because it is a good conductor of electricity. However, electricity has a more difficult time flowing through the strand of steel wool. This makes it heat up and break apart. Fuses also have a thin strand of wire in them. If something goes wrong with an electric circuit, the wire in the fuse heats up and melts, breaking the circuit and stopping the flow of electricity. This prevents an accident, such as a fire, from occurring.

4 To Conduct Or Not

What Conducts Electricity?

What You Need:
- strip of cardboard
- scissors
- 2 large paper clips
- 3 pieces of insulated wire
- light socket (mini cleat receptacle)
- 6-volt light bulb
- 6-volt battery

What You Do:

First

1. Cut the cardboard into a strip about 3 inches by 8 inches.
2. Make two slits in the cardboard about 6 inches apart and just long enough for the paper clips to slide through.
3. Attach a paper clip to the end of each wire.
4. Slide each paper clip through the slit in the cardboard so that about half the paper clip is showing through.
5. Attach one of the wires from a paper clip to the screw on the light socket.
6. Attach the other wire from the paper clip to one of the battery terminals.
7. Attach the third wire from the light socket to the remaining battery terminal.

Next

1. Gather several objects such as a pencil, string, scissors, and a plastic ruler to test their conductivity.
2. Place each object across the paper clips ensuring that both ends of the object touch the paper clips.

3. Observe the light bulb.

What Happens:
Some objects cause the light bulb to go on, and some do not.

What It Proves:
Some materials conduct electricity better than others. That means, some materials make it easier for electrons to flow through the substance. Items such as wood and plastic are poor conductors of electricity. They cannot complete the circuit to allow the electricity to flow. Other items, such as copper, are better conductors and allow the electricity to freely flow through the circuit.

5 Quiz Me

Can You Make Your Own Electric Game?

What You Need:
- piece of stiff cardboard
- sharp pencil
- 10 paper fasteners
- 8 pieces of insulated wire
- light socket (mini cleat receptacle)
- 6-volt light bulb
- 6-volt battery

What You Do:

First

1. Think up five fun questions to stump your friends. Write the questions in a column along the left side of the cardboard.
2. Write the answers in a different order from the questions in a column on the right side of the cardboard.
3. With a sharp pencil, make a hole through the cardboard next to each question and answer.
4. Push the paper fasteners through each of the holes and bend back the legs.
5. Attach one end of a wire to the leg of a paper fastener from a question and the other end of the wire to the leg of the fastener that is the question's answer.
6. Repeat the procedure until all questions and answers have been wired.
7. Attach the remaining wires to the battery and light socket as shown in the diagram.

Next

Have your friends answer the questions by placing one wire on the fastener of the question and the other wire on the correct answer.

What Happens:
If your friend answers the question right, the light bulb will turn on. If he or she answer incorrectly, the light bulb will not turn on.

What It Proves:
Electricity needs to flow through a complete circuit. When your friend answers a question correctly, the electricity flows through the wires. When the answer is incorrect, the circuit is still broken and the electricity cannot flow.

LAW LIBRARY

IF YOU'RE GOING TO TRY A CASE IN MY COURTROOM, YOU'D BETTER BE PREPARED. IF YOU'RE IN DOUBT, CHECK IT OUT . . . AT THE LAW LIBRARY.

Fact Check

- Electricity was first discovered by the Greeks in about 600 BC. The type of electricity discovered was later called *static electricity*.
- An electric current was first generated in 1831 by Michael Faraday.
- The first battery was made in 1800 by an Italian scientist, Alessandro Volta. He discovered that some metals and a liquid could work together to produce electricity.
- The electric measurement called the *volt* was named after Allessandro Volta.
- A light bulb works in the same way a fuse does. Electricity flows into the light bulb and passes through a thin wire called a *filament*. The electricity has to push hard to get through the wire. This makes the wire hot and it begins to glow with a bright light.
- Samuel Morse invented a way to send messages by means of electrical signals in 1838. He developed a code of long and short sounds or flashes of light which represented the letters of the alphabet. This system of communication became known as the Morse Code.
- Electricity is our most useful source of energy and power. It can be changed into other forms of energy including heat, sound, and light.

Buzz Words

battery—a device that stores electricity

circuit—the complete path along which an electric current flows

conductor—a material that allows electric current to flow through it

electric current—the flow of electrons through a substance

electron—a tiny particle of an atom that has a negative electric charge

galvanometer—an instrument used to detect the existence of small electric currents

insulator—a material that does not allow electrons to flow through it

parallel circuit—an electric circuit where several objects, such as light bulbs, are connected one after another so that electricity goes through each one

voltmeter—an instrument used to measure electrical pressure

volt—a unit used to measure the amount of pressure in an electric circuit